THE FEATHER-LIST EXTRACTS

just keep leaving me
notes on pianos

from *The Sentimental ABC*

THE FEATHER-LIST
EXTRACTS

Charles Johnson

EDITED BY DAVID HART

Five Seasons Press 2005

Published May 2005 by
Five Seasons Press
41 Green Street
Hereford HR1 2QH · UK

www.fiveseasonspress.com
books@fiveseasonspress.com

ISBN 0 947960 37 6

Designed & typeset in Jenson
at Five Seasons Press
and printed on
Five Seasons recycled paper
(paper specification/polemic page 128)
by MPG Books Ltd
Bodmin Cornwall UK

Front cover design by Charles Johnson

Five Seasons acknowledges
financial assistance from

for
Philippa
& Thomas Alfie

A tremendous catalogue of gratitude to those who have taught and encouraged me, most obviously

David, Gillian, Glenn, Jane, Janie, Jennifer, Joan, Joyce, Matthew, Roger, Tom and Wendy (not counting Hildegard of Bingen and Meister Eckhart)

Poems or earlier versions of poems in this collection have appeared in the following publications

Beyond Bedlam (Anvil, 1997), Blade, Brando's Hat, Braquemard, Fire, Headlock, Helicon, Leaves at the World's Edge (Bishop's Castle Community College, 1997), Listen (Flarestack, 1999), Lodestones (The Border Poets, 2001), Meridian Anthology of Contemporary Poetry vol. 11 (NM Cyprian Publishers, Naples, Florida, 2004), Navis, Needs be (Flarestack, 2000), Poems for the Waiting Room, Psychopoetica, Raw Edge, Silly fuss over a dragon (Hereford Poetry Group, 1998), Smoke, Spokes, Tears in the Fence, The Frogmore Papers, The Land Songs (Flarestack, 2003), The Magazine, The Path from the Year's Height (The Border Poets, 1999), The Rialto, Working Titles

Contents

Introduction

Anyone who finds or is found by this book will need no persuading of its invigorating provocations and pleasures. But a book that has come by packhorse many hard local miles should have a flagwaver, and I am glad to be here in the middle of the track with a flag-note. It has come to seem obvious that such poems have earned a place together in one book. Some have appeared in anthologies, some in magazines, many have been buried under the piles of other people's poems, poems Charles has been generously publishing both in the magazine, *Obsessed With Pipework*, and in individual collections. For myself, entertained, significantly puzzled and instructed as I have been for many years by Charles's writing, I have wanted these poems in one place. Selecting the poems with him and putting them into sections, their variety has become even more apparent, their taking on new tasks—often it seems without his even knowing what the task was; their creeping up on what matters or might matter—a rare lateral-thinking gift, this—and their standing up to—responding newly to—repeated readings, makes for a book that can now show what he's been up to and to what magical purpose. Not least, watch how words work here, how language gate-crashes thought, how thought is taken for unexpected walks with language, and how, if there is a gene for wry humour, it is surely showing itself here. Who knows what anyone will be reading fifty years from now? We work in our laboratories, poems happen, they find their way in the world, now, later.

David Hart
Birmingham
January 2005

INCUNABLES

Dad at Cerne

Half the time
the old man's mind
is trying to fight free of some thicket
like a blind man in brambles.
He hears what you say but the half of it
won't sink in.

Every month
when the moon lets him climb
he's off up that hill
and sleeps along the Rude Man's long member
or spends the night watching the stars
to get back his manhood.

Half the time
when he comes home,
his back wet with dew,
he's singing.

A trompe-l'œil drawn on glass

Look, from this spot by the window-seat (stoop a little,
close one eye) the effect is all but perfect:
the smaller statues are more distant
though the sides of the path are not right—
they should meet at the end of the vista.

Couples converse by the parterre. Their shadows
appear to be painted on the gravel:
they do not fade when clouds obscure
the sun. Their owners seem able
to walk away & leave them.

To move your head even an inch, or undo the latch
would spoil the deception. Those squirrels
that ripple & twitch alongside the maze
 are too quick to have shadows—
greys, they are a recent introduction.

The dancers in period costume
on what was once the bowling green
are real. Listen & you will hear
faintly, through the glass, restored sackbuts
& serpents playing in the orchard.

Low Sunday weeding

What was all the birds'
fuss at half past four
this morning? Jesus
April knocked
winter into a cocked hat
before it dawned on me
Easter's been again.

Look at the mess: undying grass
everywhere untidies the dead
neatness cold months left. Even here
in our thumbnail lawn
young sun's begun
planting its randy lions, heraldic golden
dandy sons to pierce the fudge-soft earth,
thudding in finger thick
tap-root darts.

Barbed feline roots tongue and poke,
show their true colours, give themselves ragged
green rosettes for effort, style, taste.
I try to tug them out—meagre
yellow parsnips' muddy crop—
if it's been wet enough, take them by surprise—
otherwise they clench in
and break off bleeding thick
bitter milk.

Just removed finger holes stud the lawn
leaving fives of warm deep leather sockets
worms and weed-seeds tumble down.
Watch spring's rocket
light the blue mathematical burning spiral
to summer's unstoppable curve.

Landscape with figures

A rich brown afternoon field curves down,
ridged as a ploughman's knee, to the track,
the corn as always too late to show;
ducks on the glassy pond look ill at ease.

It's still and quiet. The light is harsh.
No birds sing in the dusty trees.
All trains here arrive or fail to arrive
at ten to three by the station clock.

The twin Miss Joneses, in pink and in black,
with nothing to do but meet each train,
stand solidly glued to the platform and wait
for ever—or for no time at all.

The station-master seems only to live
to chat to the man by the churns and the truck.
Always unstable, the porter fell under
the last Up express. He's away being mended.

We call this the day room

Have you ever been here? A full
empty day high as a room,
grey, bland—a whole tall
square of air to inhale
before another bed-time.

Can you see our view?
Look at the little willow and the black
trees like hands, severe, cut back.
See the paint peel
on the pale disregarded gazebo.

Do you like jigsaws? This one's
all there, according to Gilbert. He's normally
an accountant, but I have my suspicions
about the big hole in the sky.
Still, it beats watching TV all day.

(Odd, how each day just one day's worth of news happens)
The empty sky is grey, and the lawns:
sometimes people stroll there, walk
their dogs through the courtyard, or talk.
It's hard to keep making them all perform.

Did you see the corridor?
I don't much care for the décor:
mosaic mares can stare up from the floor
by the hatch where we wait for our medication.
In the wallpaper I sometimes see Buddhas or toads seeking satori.

Dismal   lament

Having done   enough work
for the week,   keen for a break
I step from the bus   sublime, beyond
where the chimney-pots   stop
at the canal.   Landing
where a vole gnaws,   swans flap
and the water   retreats and returns,
I resolve to throw   worries away
in my euphoria.   Aircraft   trails   slicing
decorative above   evolve into
a white and blue   eulogy.
With an air of languor,   roughshod girls,
one tall in the extreme,   emerge
lighting cigarettes,   setters at heel.
One has a cool   look,
refined,   denying attraction,
my heart   tragically burns
for the other,   rehearses overtures,
waxes   sexual: I could,
if I were taller,   relate to her,
become   emotional, but this urge
my hormones   send
is deemed   demented, doomed
to remain unrequited   deterred by her height.

Crophead

for Carrington 'Queen of Nothing'

I have seen you standing in the pasture
beyond the ha-ha, feet, in those silly shoes
with the ankle laces, placed at ten past ten
on grass that looks like straw, your pigeon-toes
not in evidence as you shade your eyes and listen
to we shall never know what as it goes
over the elms or the house—aeroplane or bird.

Late summer, from the cut look of the field
and your tanned shoulders. Sun-streaked head
of bronze hair as always cropped, belled
to lay bare the lobes of your ears, the cleft
of your nape. Your eyes, they say, were oddly pale
and I guess I know what that means, a look as if
bleached by the sun, by the light,
by too much looking and too much salt
shed in your bed for lost lovers over the years.

Poem for (to) from, by/my mother

O dear, son
I don't seem, do I, to have
explained things very well,
taught you how to live?
I guess that's because
I don't know—does anyone?

       ~

I only seem to have
one authentic memory
of my mother, maybe two:
how her whole hips jiggled
at the stove when she beat eggs;
how that disturbed me in my teens.
And her dreadful ankles like an ostrich's.

Otherwise there are family stories
that may or may not be true, and maybe one more:
her answering my question why emery boards were kept
in the Singer drawer with the old needles
(to clean any rust off that might stop
them slipping through the material).

      ~

These are the stories—
the last: that she passed away peacefully
just as she'd sat down for a meal
'with the grandchildren around her' ;

the first: in that historic bad winter of January 1947
when I should have started school but the snow
was so thick she wasn't going to send me

(though she didn't tell me that)
until I made such a fuss she dragged me there
by the hand all the way past buried railings.

In between, how many stories?
—Picasso allowed to paint faces
with both eyes one side of the nose
because he'd learned to draw properly first.

—*Why did you tie my beloved cat to the stool*
with your school tie?
He only dragged it all the way along
the pink hall lino to the foot of the stairs.

—*Wait until your father gets home*

—Having to apologise for calling her an old bag,
not knowing how rude it was.

It's all right, Mum. I'm sure
there's nothing to explain
that can be explained
but can you tell me
the meaning of these pictures?

Paternity

My two sisters and I
had I think three fathers
but because we never thought
to ask him who he was
before it was too late
before the chess board was put away
and the strange uncles called for the last time
to honour our mother
now we'll never know.

Funny the things you notice

You'd lost some weight but you looked well.
You had on
a pale grey suit, kind of shiny, and you'd had
your hair trimmed—not like you.
At some point you wore your French helmet
and read us some poems. You read them
as if they were jokes. So many books—
thin books with dull-coloured covers, books
you would bring home second-hand on pay day.

I thought some were by Enright, but later
when I went back expecting to find them
the book-case was empty, fresh-painted blue-grey.
Just a hand-written note on a half-sheet
of torn blue-lined paper 'Poems P'.

On birthdays you would tell us we could go
and find surprise presents in the piano stool.
You never bothered to wrap them. My sister
has your RAF photo now, black waves showing
under the cap you wore at that angle, grinning
in front of an aircraft engine, by the smooth
fat rubber tyre, shoulder-high, slashed with streaks
of what looks like varnish but must be fresh oil.
The buttoned pockets with the pleats.

When she and I meet we remember how we were
as a family. All this misses you.

Looking for Floodgate Street

Dark men walk along
in the crime district, some
take home pistols in Tesco bags,
some carry the latest style
of lampshade
their wife insists on,
some have greyhounds,
some meat pies.

Buddleias bloom galore
among the motorbikes
parked in the nub end
of Paternoster Row.

Barn Street, Milk Street,
Little Ann Street—dear dead Dad,
what are you trying to tell me,
leading me through
the hot metal smells of Digbeth
to find a phantom gunsmith?

THE DAUGHTER POEMS

Name tracing

Long out of season, cold and bored
the sea slaps petulant
against the front—
a wilful child ignored.

Across the sand-silted prom
I hunch in the library's salt-bleared window
puzzle down lists, look for a name,
a street; attract no attention.

Through vast acoustic stations
where litter twirls to empty tunes
I have come on a quest
whose motive you choose to distrust.

Later, finished, overdue for coffee,
crossing deserted public gardens
the sun is leaving fast,
I almost collide with a black lamp-post.

I shall get home hungry
but better than never,
with the gift of a daughter
in the world once more.

My daughter the deer

What do you do when your daughter
turns into a horse
and a bird

when you find you've turned into
a cow
when your mother's turned into another
kind of bird?

And what do you do when
your husband's turned into a tree
your son has turned into a plank
when your lover's turned into the wind
and blown away?

You stay clear of the blind spot behind
and you look out old blankets and sew
you watch out for her moods
and your mind.

One star left

I could make the clouds you call for
out of what torn-off stamps
leave on parcel paper.

The world is full of voices. Every wardrobe
from here to New South Wales has a quota
of padded bags, folded brown strata, bubble-wrap

ready to send
a gift for a friend,
a lover

a disconnected daughter.
Christmases slip forward faster
than I'd have thought it possible
to blink, let alone be getting on with a life.
The only response I can manage is a giggle

and to sit an hour by the water
in the heart of the Manchester she owns
with my niece, enjoy her laughter

pretend she's my child (there's a family cast to her features
despite the adopted Scots accent)
wonder how she looks to her undoubted lovers.

The Depth of Field dilemma and the hooks

When for my project: Hotels Toilets of America
I focus my Pentax
with the close-up filter
on the nearer
of the twin chrome hooks back of the lavatory door,
wherever does the further
prong go as I watch it blur
away to nothing in the glass box
of the viewfinder?

It can't be nowhere,
can't that moment cease
to exist in any sense,
simply chooses absence,
to cover its tracks,
seem to disappear
like the cleverer daughter.

I should maybe say Shallowness: a paradox.

DYKE

Dawn by the water

Light on the water that eerie greenish,
brighter than the sky.

There's a jangle of harness
as the seaweed man's horse
sneezes into his feedbag. The breeze
freshens up from the mudflats
thinning the white fog. We wait
for the first boat home
to the asylum on the island.

On the ghost of a borrowed bicycle
the drains inspector rattles past
late from a night at the opera.
Leant up against the breakwater
her hat on back to front
the ringmaster's alcoholic mother
keeps pretending not to nod off.

An editorial cleverness
for Roger Garfitt at 52

Easy to say *as we all do,*
but you seem to exist
extradimensionally, at once
now and twenty years ago—
taking a stand in magazines
for the unforced, the fragile;
teaching us older learners
what to cultivate, to watch for;
to keep us patrolling
the borderlands. And so
back to your own ground
where you now seem as much
part of the tradition as angel
jester or ploughman
carved on a misericord:
vital, unassuming, prone
to be overlooked, sat upon.

At Walcot

Hands folded together
I'm not even bothering to look up to where
I know the tree hardly moves
outside the closed window.

Logs settle. I wait
for nothing to happen.
Just the turquoise wall
and the cherry red settee.

The shoes of the lion
at Llanthony in the Black Mountains
for Glenn

I want luminous paint
to make a skeleton
in cardboard
for the back of the door
of your cupboard,

a mask, a picture
where I become a buzzard
for easy travel to other places
under a stand of high heron-coloured clouds

if bear claws
or eagle quills
might give a wild heart

a venerable pair
of blotting-paper boots
—a publisher's indian gift—
lend the spirit of the lion

quilt-soft bilberries
to float on under nothing
but the sky; black tarns size of a bed
reflect nothing and wait to take you down
to a world where lost men wake in the dark
and wonder if it's time

fast footwear to soar
up the rocky hill
past aged bright thorn trees
to the high marshy edge
where white and purple dragons hang
in English cloud
over ordered counties.

To the vintage show

We turn in here at the orange arrows,
barely notice we squash through
a gutter awash
with small bitter apples.

This end of the sloping field
smells of crushed grass,
gently shudders, green with paint
oily-rag-wiped to a sheen.

Fair to see, the region's rejuvenated
two-strokes putter,
pumping nothing in particular from a to b
for the pride of it.

Behind a rope young owners have drawn up
a few fifty-year-old vans
waxed bright as yellow pre-packed peppers,
red as autumn hawthorns.

So who restored
the hedgerow's damsons, then, this year,
lacquered the blackberries,
polished the sloes?

The Fourth Book of Humours

Winter. Vivaldi makes
his frantic fiddlers slow and show
the locking-up of moisture,
drying of blood.

Meat becomes first cheap, then scarce;
dear, then hard to find.

Only a few beasts, the breeders,
remain, live as family. All else
are smoked and salted away.
Dry bread, peas, beans, meal
and fire come into their own.

Fuel is found, garnered,
comes out, runs out. At the depth
of this hard time, after the madness
of bonfires, desperation.

No-one ventures
abroad; the sickly die.

Conservation rules
and the fear: what if this one year
the sun fails to halt and turn back
from his own decline?

This one book packs away
within its suit of meanings
resting, waiting, all the rest.

THE GOING POEMS

Christmas night in the warehouse

Determined to remain the outsider, not to do
the hackneyed thing, you walk out
before the cold weather; spend the holiday season
in the locked-up offices.

Bedtime at dusk, not daring to show a light.
Once the office door was bolted
the police wouldn't bother.

Porridge on the staffroom ring,
cocoa with evap, Ryvita with spreads.

You become for those few quiet days
an ecologist of the life of the pavements, expert on
who goes to the city centre newsagents at five a.m.

Don't do it at Christmas

You're supposed to stick it out, stay together
for Christmas, walk out if you must at New Year's.

Sleeping in the car. Christmas with the pigeons in the square.
Breakfast at New Street. Bedtime reading at New Street
till they lock up at 2 a.m. Walk the streets till they re-open at 4.

Wait for something to turn up—get a flat—stick it out—
give up—go back—carry on again as if it's okay.
Go back to work. Dodge the cleaners. Hide
in the washroom till everyone's gone.
Don't have the grace to tell her
where you are.

LOCUS

My flat feels too small

I made France and the Low Countries out of pillows,
that whole sweep from Portugal and Gibraltar down to Greece
from an old blanket with stripes near the edge,
putting cushions under places I might land,
and threw myself into Europe, another place
broken by two sadnesses.

There was a little pain below my elbow
but I managed to make Newark Airport,
or it might have been O'Hare,
at a friend's house in the next town, which may be too far,
and Ireland at the village bakery when it was open
smelling of hundreds-and-thousands and ham
so there could be a break in the flight with croissants.

My stepson finished demonstrating the computer
to my new woman poet friend. They moved on
to consider the ironing board.
To get post from the lobby I had to go
through the back door and walk round.
I made a sign through the glass to them not to close it.
They would have shut me out.

I had to move toys from the floor
and decided some birds on the lawn
under the seed feeder could be the Balearics.
I wondered about the fate of the children,
whether they had entered the rock.

Has the bull gone?

O magic city, comfortable city!
where the swans (a swan)
still cruise the cool dark canal
and look up at me on the bridge
looking down at 40 years ago, 50
and in his bedroom someone's practising
cornet scales like I used to
only better.

The Co-op stables have gone
& the Co-op steam laundry,
but Sunleigh Grove's still there,
where we started to learn
to use matches.

I missed the Journey's End
at the bottom of Clay Lane
but the kids on the Dell
on the way to the crem
said it's still there.

The Rover's gone
where they used to make tanks
but the low circular castles are there
round the oak trees I remember
taught me with acorns.
And the 44 bus terminus clock.
The importance of time
& how it doesn't matter—lessons
I forget time
& time again.

I wonder where he's gone

If I were to read my diary I'd find
a whacking great leaf-green grasshopper and I
found each other in a cheap hotel in France.
The morning was dull, the two maids were vacuuming,
emptying ashtrays and bundling sheets in our rooms.

He was outside on the windowledge
to give me delight and a story.
Did he see me? Did I reach out
and catch him? No. I didn't know
I'd find I needed him but I find
in a strange way I've brought him to show you.

A hot night at the *Fronton*

What are these shouts that wake me
singing *Ay Jalisco*
each time I fall towards my dream?

The young men playing jai alai
are agile and quick like wasps.
Their curved rackets twirl,
graceful but poised for a blow
like my heart twisting and hurling
away from you.

Maria is dancing with the passion of a woman
not yet married. The young girls envy her anger.
She is remembering she married the window cleaner
when she could have had the butcher.

The wicker slings strapped to the players' wrists
twist like the white sails of dhows crossing river shallows,
the curved horns of a browsing group of oryx
or the dancing head-dresses of three or four nuns
trying to hold a conversation as they negotiate
a busy shopping street
in a stiffish breeze as rain starts.

He will not wash her kitchen window because of the wasps.
The melon skins on the rubbish heap bring them,
and all the orange peel my neighbour puts out.

They catch and scoop the hard ball, steady,
turn, swish and slam it at the wall,
detonate dust-pocks.

A Tune a Day

for my Sally Ann cornet

A different kind of pipework.
Little bottle brush for cleaning the tubes
and every bend detachable,
able to be cleaned and polished.

Each valve unscrews so I can oil it.

A leaf shaped mend where a little chunk of silver
has been soldered in place on the side of the bell
and the unforgiving brass cup
always thirsty for the purse of my lips.

What does he think I'm doing?
Every week I go on two buses to pay to be scorned
for not doing my practice to a man over a music shop in Brum
who runs a dance band. On the side
he makes a fool of me & my ambitions.

I want to be Miles Davis,
Bob Brookmeyer or the man on my EP
who plays Blue Turning Grey Over You
and breaks my heart for any other music.

Bunking off work

There is something in the air:
time may be opening or closing
a tall stone door somewhere

and sleeping has become a problem:
the middle-aged fool finds himself
at 4.30 pulling faces in the dark room,
trying to make out what he's here for

so through that strange morning
the smooth blood-red car (that clearly bears
the spirit of the caribou and the skin drum)
is seen parked here and there around the city
at sites where the goddess might still
talk to him by a diverted stream

while he looks for a sign
in how rain running down
café windows cuts up the view
of seats in the garden;
the sudden low flight of geese
from the boat lake; the pattern
in puddles by the bridge; how
the photos of undertakers line
the red corridor.

He takes back to his room
that is filling with paints
he doesn't expect now to use
a cheap CD with one Carly Simon track
he wants to hear "I know
nothing stays the same"
and is grouchy to his wife.

THE NEW YORK CITY POEMS

Seven ten AM

If I look down
from my hotel
I can see across the street
white shoes, white socks
on a walking machine
already working up a sweat
in the third floor corner gym.

The sky above Columbus

(or the UN—it's the same)
invisibly strikes down
like one of Gutenberg's dies
between the grey thin branches
at the edge of the park,
the East River.

WALKing across 57th Street

This morning I saw a single sparrow
in a bare tree—no, you don't understand:
first bird I'd noticed all week
since the seagulls high over Cooper-Hewitt.

Poem it's best stays unfinished

You know something? I've been seriously stuck,
but I only saw it as I almost bought
(at the Newark Airport Hudson News) new copies
of *Franny & Zooey* and *Seymour, an introduction.*
Phrases convince me they're exhumed word for word
from Salinger's folded and refolded text—the ten year old letter
Buddy reads in the bath 'on the two dry islands of his knees'.

Each time has its texture

Let me give you the taste of my week. The wind
blew off the sea. In the book I was reading
one Marco da Sola came to Oxford from Venice
by way of the shifting shallows
of Restoration London. We slept late.

Our oranges arranged themselves on the caravan table.
We ate damp ham sandwiches
next to Pembroke Castle. Rabbits danced
with jackdaws, shops sold me talismans and a new comb.
Purple foxgloves waved high along the lanes,
all night tankers waited in the dark in the bay
for the tide to reach Milford. We drank
from clear aquamarine plastic cups and the wind blew off the sea.

Most days I drew hexagrams that spoke of waiting,
contemplating paths I tend to turn a blind eye to. I climbed
the headland, met a fox at the top, got caught
in a muddy field, washed my shoes on the beach,
and the wind blew off the sea.

Views from Hotels part two

This morning Mrs Kodaly's two grey yard alsatians
are silent in their Škoda kennel next to the hotel.
Ex-communist high-rises backdrop the motorway.
Everything in sight is in need of repair
or unfinished or both, except the trees
& the birds & the grass and the powder-blue house
with the porthole windows, white brick chimneys
& a spanking red van.

The hanky-size orchard next door sports a washing line
pegged with a junior crusader team strip.
Eliphas Bodnar in jama bottoms tiptoes
a frying pan right to the end of his garden
to water his marrows. None of this
approaches Kafka.

Breakfast spinach scents the air by the desultory tram-queue.
Street names are on cardboard in case they need changing.
Every garden in this street where the blackbirds are calling
has a dog.

Further on smells of railing-paint red over brown.
Cut grass or the lime trees. The purple and blue
freightyard wildflowers put up their shutters for the day
when the heat starts at 9.17. Incomprehensible
posters are sellotaped to the telegraph poles—
cement ones with those oval holes all the way up.
How to capture the flowers at each windowledge and pushing
through the railings in a country where the wage
is 200 a month?

Dad taught me Charlie Forest is an oilstone

Shade means under leaves.
Wet rocks.
Grey becomes brown.
Brown means the colour of Keswick slate that concentrates
in heavy squareish blocks each a fistful
like expensive chocolate
in the shallow edge of Lake something
(you have to tell me
the name again: Bassenthwaite).

Some of the slate is in grey blades split
perfectly flat one side like arrow flakes.
Rubbing them together like a madman sharpening a stone knife
minutes at a time with water
makes a silvery paste that behaves like paint.
It's a thing I do
when I don't know what to do
near the edge of a dark cloud.

What if it rains the whole fortnight?

The first few waves
back of the neverending edge of the sea
run purple enough to bottle—

dark and dense as flint
lend the ocean an edge
chipped with white.

Ahead of their shaving
sky chromes wet sand
mercurial blue.

The drums of the longshore wind
are speaking to me deep below the applause
of the receding tide. What they speak of
too dark for words—their thunders go beyond
the who the when
the how the if & the daydreams
to a place of wordless certainties
where I'm rooted to the world beyond world—
tell me of my invisible track on the beach
that is broad as the ocean and mine.

O Painswick

O Stroud, O Nailsworth
you can be heartbreaking
hills, blindfolded horses
in fields going steep
to the river valley
where we no longer find
the mythic piano mill.

Lost through the muddy woods.
Gun shops, bookstall just there
for me to meet
Rilke, Kafka, learn how
to heal my life,
treat my heart more kindly.

Wooden plates with landscapes
that flow across them
and seas in the sky.

I expect we bought them with our choirboy
wedding shillings

They were American motorbike cops
They were probably from Woolworth's
They could well have come
from the factory that made water pistols
Someone had designed them
Someone had set up the machines
Someone had carefully chosen the shade
of clear green plastic
so we expected them to taste
like lime-flavoured boiled sweets
There was a mouthpiece at the back
and a thing in the wheels
whizzed round with a sireny kazoo sound when you blew

They were a wonderful toy
allowing the breath
to make a present for the ear
like a poem does

If you picked up the cathedral
and blew hard into the porch
a suitably-sized pea in the chapter house
would whiz round too
but I can't think if the sound
would be the voice of God

Settling in at Damsel's Farm

We played Can't Hurry Love in the car on the way.
Heaven might be here, deep between southward spurs
in this secret box of air where the track could be crumbled cheese,
clouds strayed from some engraving fail to tangle in the cedar,
and you can't see the farmhouse from the lane.

The front door once tarred has weathered pale as driftwood.
Willow-grey lamb's tongue wilts round the mallow where they're
        trying
to start a garden by the wall that flakes red beneath the chestnut.
A young sheep so tame we guess it's hand-reared
stands and lonelily rolls *lehrer* round its tongue.

The elm-bole lies sun-bleached, nettle-garrisoned, wormed by time
and weather; mother to flat loaves of fungus, too, twisted
like a wrung-out mummy rag of river turbulence. Those bees
that boil a mirage round their entrance are not hostile,
but how friendly is it when a meadow horsefly stabs your hand?

The staircase smells of laundry, polish, lemons, Earl Grey.
Dark doorknobs loosely jangle and the long landing boards
knock, tracking visitors' overhead moves through the day.

In the passage to the room is framed a second question: are lapwing
and peewit the same? At the back of the house stone mullions
bracket a plump horse tossing tail & mane in the wind on the hillside.
Late sunlight reddens his innocent behind.

The Absentminded Man
and the angel he's allowed to call Miss Voss
on the tomb of the brother-in-law of Mr Gladstone
have a little chat

Just noticed I've hurt my finger
as the workmen in eighteen doodle dum
must have hurt themselves sometimes
lugging these slabs of marble brought by horsecart
—and I imagine all the stomping hooves, hot snorting breath,
the rattle and crunch of iron-hooped wheels on cobbles
the harmony or clash of all sorts and conditions of men.

Did the marble come from round here—not Italian, surely,
even for such a notable with an angel at each corner?
The other three seem brain-dead, but you
so calm and spiritual—a little stick of marble
(or is it alabaster?) saw it all
—the sweating and straining, the doffed caps, the boots,
the masons' hardened hands, the ladies
under these columns and arches.

The sepulchre designer's sleepless nights,
the reputations at stake, the early rising to see to the horses,
the signing for work performed, the careful shaving, the brushing
of hair, the payment of accounts. The bills. The tradesmen.

The black bombazine, the silk, the linen,
the straw and sacking, the stone-dust,
the shovels and crowbars, the levers and shoving
you heard. The ring of a chisel dropped
on the hard tiles. No wonder the floor's worn.
And all to get this worthy man into
his proper Victorian place
in Worcester's heaven.

Being here

I have not yet tasted the stream. So silly
to have been here a whole week
and not touched the water.
How can I hope to do any good writing
if I don't even put my hand in the cold?

Light silvers the shallows
like I knew it would
and I notice that
but who needs to be told?
The grass is silvered too.
There are no dead cows in the river,
no skulls in the field
that I can see. The bramble leaves
have turned red, and my eye
enjoys seeing that
so much I half-heartedly
risk drawing blood
to pick a stalk.

A long shadow starts
with its feet at my wellingtons,
its head over there by the hedge.
Coins left on the trees
almost few enough to count.
Caught out by the morning, the moon
that sails over the lane
seems upside down.

Coming from a country without cabbages

Rosamund tells me my camellia
wants acid thrown over it sometimes.
I dream of lemons and think of a gardener
offering me crystals, a kind of blue salt.
It may be each month, it may only be
on the first of July, in September
and again before the fireworks.

The leaves are a little unwell—
shiny as though just lacquered
and still wet, bringing to mind
the papier-mâché of my mother's table,
its flowers painted on flakes of shell.
I feel its lightness, the crust soft as pastry.
It could have been black treacle
with the heart of a lion, dead
but the skin unbroken,
full of bees.

The buds drop before they have opened,
already foxed in brown. It misses its home.
I picture France or Spain,
a place with lizards, earth with no lime.
I will move its pot to the shade of the green bin
where my worms live, the orange slugs,
the six thousand ants, my tiny flies.
I will keep it aloof from the soil,
worry for it.

THE HEARTLAND POEMS

Healing with more than cobwebs & honey

the doktor wears a mask
the petiant wears a mask
both could do
with a spell-czech

carotid
doppler
ultrasound
I've had 2 letters—one a month ago said
taking pictures of your body using sound waves
please have nothing to eat or drink for eight hours
hand this letter to the receptionist
some jelly will be placed on the part
in question— o
WILL THERE BE CANDLES?
GAMES? PRESENTS? A BAG
TO TAKE HOME? *Please drink*
1½ pints of clear fluids
do not empty your bladder

now this one saying *come;*
write poems
with a map showing car parks
could be St Petersburg
or a proud Renaissance city
could be either, could be both

Having seen only the map
the letters of introduction
I've seen cities before
other cities
what do I expect?

Anticipating Heartlands

You posted me a plan with the car parks
didn't narrow down what I expected
overmuch. The bird's eye looks down
on medieval Venice streets
of leaning palaces could well be
a concentration of cell blocks
Moscow University or a downtown
department store district out of Orwell
or even an artist's reconstruction
of the ruins of Ur of the Chaldees.
I'm not a patient. Why does it scare me?

The smartie hat

A virgin cardboard vomit bowl—they double as party hats—
gets filled from newly-opened packs with smarties and maltesers
and left at the nurses' station by a serious lady in white.
I somehow hesitate to ask
this wordless ritual act's significance
till the tea trolley comes. It turns out she's a consultant
—the only one who does this.
It turns out it's to try to brighten people's day.

A morning at A & E: at least it's not Friday night

The day before Guy Fawkes'—it's tomorrow
the fireworks start in earnest—it seems the team
are not 'dreading' tomorrow night as I'd have guessed
before I saw the stuff they are made of: they say
the evenings all run together, but Fridays are the worst

A & E signs

34 yellow one two three—
we just count the numbers down
so we know.

In the doctors' station a box
on top of the monitor
labelled 'Head Injury Audit
begins 1-10-99'

By the phones
       Porters 348
       Bleep 349
       ECG 737

All these girls in white
seem to carry in their hands
and put down all over
the desk little reels of
tape 3M micropore
like talismans. A sign
on a side-room door
DON'T PUT PILLOWS
IN HERE!

A & E extras

A lady with a mop and bucket
passes through with that
reassuring clean, healthy
smell, like part
of the scenery. Later a hum

as she hovers past again
(I recognise the air

of calm concentration)
with the quiet red polishing machine.

A painter
with a step ladder
and a brushful
of wet paint emerges
from Resuscitation.

The calm lady passes back by
with a blue broom
shepherding litter
and bits out
through the door.

Op 34 Labyrinth Test,

says the sign on the door;
Op 37 Campimetry, Op 35 Store.
We're in a backwater. Dead
red lights say Room In Use.
There are helpline posters
and a basket of bold plastic toys.

Meg Ryan comes to mind: 'better get out of here
or Security will think you're a psych patient'

This is a waiting room. While you wait
you could do something useful in your head
like get on with your life. Your name
will be called soon enough.

Chairs, doorframes and carpet
are in hints of tasteful blue
like the walls and the sky.
Sitting on the blue chairs
seems part of the treatment.

In case of fire

Do not even entertain the idea of writing
a letter to inform the fire brigade.

Do not attempt to extinguish a fire however small
with body fluids—saliva, perspiration or pee.
You would only hurt yourself.

If, however, you were brought up in a home
where the expression of feelings was frowned on
you may have a backlog of tears, even tears
of laughter or joy. These can be effective
in quenching quite large conflagrations.

6.30 pre-op

Hum, this looks a pleasant planet.
Absolutely crazy about things
I can do with no more light than spills
from the nurse's station. Being part
of this building that sails
in a world of its own through the night.

I've had the two buttered squares of white toast
I'm allowed for breakfast. Sunlight the colour
of expensive grapefruit lights the ward
from a pink sky over Coventry. They're still
having problems with the one
blood pressure machine.
Mr Bekesz could easily be taken
for Field Marshall Lord Montgomery of Alamein.
He looks worse before his op than I hope to after mine.

The water supply's labelled NOT FOR DRINKING.
The theatre gown is 45% polyester, made in Jordan
for the Standard Textile Co Inc, Cincinnati, Ohio
45237.

Doing their best

Will they have been here since before 8 o'clock
drinking strong coffee, discussing
how best to deal with us, making
last minute notes, realising they'll
never be perfectly ready,
wishing they'd had more time?

If only they could have had
the day off, stayed in bed
& let someone else handle today.
They know we're here now waiting
for them to see us, and they're worried.
Let's be kind to them, hey?

DUENDES

My Dear Writing . . .

[1] Hardly recognised you this morning

I hate that you ask so much of me—that I feel
I should get up at three every night & fill pages for you.
And yet what you give me is so much more
than enough.

I can't call you beautiful and seem sincere,
but you are. You have days
you should stay in your room
—but oh
when you're calm & relaxed & at ease
what a knockout! I would die just to serve you.

Slopping in jeans and a top:
a slumming princess gussied up to the nines
with nail varnish & scent. By tea-time a slattern once more,
you tease me pretending to wear
someone else's ring, to prove
(a) your power
(b) I care—and I do
but the clincher's for my sins you're still mine all mine.

[2] Look, I know you're there somewhere
it's no use pretending
you're a tree
or putting on a red nose and trip-up shoes.
The essential Grace Kelly shines through with a style
I would know anywhere.

[3] I'm in charge since I really enjoy
spending nights on the fire stairs
too much wine
and a sky full of stars.

THE FISH POEMS

Looking at the tank in the morning dark

Hardly any fish have died lately, in fact
checking the calendar it's been more than a month,
not counting the crab.

But what will happen if I come to see you?

The nitrite level has been higher than I like
for a few days, and this morning is around
2 parts per million, as if they knew something.

Can we talk? I don't want fish on my conscience.

Converses with catfish about mirrors

I'm not due in Worcester till ten
and the muesli's doing in the blue microwave
but I come in to tell my black Widows
(and Corydoras julii if he's awake)
the birdbath's frozen solid so it'll take
a good five minutes scraping ice from Rose
before I feel she's safe to drive.
I didn't mean to make you cry again.

*Macropodus opercularis Sunday morning with Gerald
Stern*

Last week the Three of Swords
with its fat scarlet heart
pierced by the polished blades
pointed towards the Empress

after the fool on the Four of Cups couldn't see
what was under his nose
and I was brave
knowing I must be strong for your sake
but now with nothing to do
but hear the paper-cart and the windy road
it's hard to leave the phone alone
make toast
get on with my books
and be wise for my peaceful paradise fish
to whom I have permitted no mate.
I suddenly remember every ruined life.

Welding Queen

I salute you, Zelda, punk transformer
of junk as you push up your blank
round-eyed goggles
to your forehead and light
yet another
Capstan Full Strength
from the turned-down
oxyacetylene jet.

Hair cropped short and variously flame,
purple, henna, black with the season,
you make few concessions to gender
yet when the mood is on you cast
a spell will not be gainsaid.
No choice then
but to be commanded
by your unspoken whim.

If I rang you (how can I ring you?) you'd be out

I made headlamps and wind to buffet the windows tonight
and bring home to me how I feel. In my dream bookshop
in the seaside town tall women with direct gazes
stare at me as bears would from the tv papers.

The wooden cottage is a ship in a storm of trees. Dotted lines
from my wife's noisy sleep rule off each total on the till roll
that accounts for the night. I could tell your machine
I'll be bringing home a book called desire.

Raindrops gossip at the glass in code. Behind me latches rattle
inarticulate thanks. Dark birds carry off the straw from our
planning stage for a cathedral. On Monday we'll maybe talk
of the beauty of certain forms of truth.

Haiku waitress

she used to relish the clasp
of the thick linen apron
doubled round her hips

autumn wind
she would murmur
as she sushied
between tables
sun becomes lazy
soon icicle at window

she may materialise
in ninja black
at stage depot
livery stables
or bank
anywhere in the badlands
and before she serves
Winchester slug,
karate chop or dynamite stick

enunciate in her own
strange tongue
confetti faces
drift on pool
koi snatch them away

her scowl is on poster trees
from here to Oregon:
WANTED
Short order waitress,
Poetry Café

THE LEAVINGS POEMS

I want to give you a table

loaded with emblems—
lute, flute, dead pheasant, nutmeg,
lead bust of cupid, astrolabe,
compass, ball of wool, ball of twine.

From the string drawer I enter the universe

I'm here but I don't want to be set free,
I just want this voice so I can tell
whoever's still awake with ears about me,
as that's the only way to transform my hell.

When I said transform I think I meant
simply evade the cognitive trap
—the box I built myself when you went
and I withdrew to my own side of life. Now I don't sleep.

I don't mean just toss & turn or count sheep:
I actually STAY AWAKE ALL NIGHT. My eyes burn
from watching the red numbers changing shape
each sixty seconds, like waiting for the phone

in a room on an empty hall in a new town
where no one knows your number. Did you come
to escape an old life or to find a new? Alone
is what you are. Could be why you left home

in the first place. First place—get it? Funny that,
how leaving home in the first place says what it means.
The trick now is to afford the flat,
to keep myself in honey, fruit & beans.

Do I need a man? I don't think so, honey
but I could do with a friend, an ear to talk to
& someone to show me the local ropes, the cunning
to survive out there while I do my heart work too.

There's no agenda, no list of instructions to follow
but I somehow think that writing it down,
my dreams and memories, what makes me want to holler
with rage & pain, will make my will return.

I know it was not your fault & you were doing
what you had to do in your turn to keep afloat
when I threatened to swamp the canoe you were rowing
in your own choppy sea. Did I calm it by going, or is it worse?

I would give you

those pictures no one bothered to take
before you went; the one Uncle Leonard
caught sight of too late
in the second before he scraped off
what he'd painted, giving up
in disgust at falling short of his vision

so you could share with your kids and their cousins
a glimpse of that startled girl
stepping out of the shower on the caravan site,
eyes pale from a summer in ray-bans

and the scary symmetrical face
of a renaissance beauty in pearls and brocade,
a skull hardly seen in the shadow beneath
the painter's symbol-laden table.

On my walk

Paying another ritual
visit to the dead
badger
above the quiet motorway
—today, he's gone
and that's somehow a relief.

I can give up making plans
to take the old kitchen knife
and bring back the head
to boil to a skull,
dog-like, for the shelf
just as I need to forget
how much I wanted you.

The burned girl

The pale girl
in chef's check trousers
and white jacket
who came across to the shop

one cheek and one eye crumpled
by we guess a kitchen fat fire
but so pretty
withal.

Returning from the locked church

Moon like a slice of lemon delighted me.
The beauty of the wind in the trees
over the path up to the church.

You wrote to ask me how I feel
about your daft idea of a book
or an MPhil in something. I want
to reply I feel angry when I'm busting
a gut to do a job I hate and you
are dilettanting about. As I pass
the buttress a security light comes on
and annoys me 'It's only me, Lord!'

A white cat like a ghost cowers
as I get back among the houses.
Then I remember Eckhart:
'Announce it, pronounce it'
and I forgive you.

Interesting weather you have here inland

This is a photo
of Miss Fiona Lestrade
as Queen of Metals. The islanders
would touch it
for protection.

She lived with her maiden sister
up at the Mansion
which was no more
than a larger turf cottage
where the mice bred. Children
would be led there.

You can make out the remains.

Living wallpaper

An enormous kitchen
luckily because
where you'd expect eye-level
cupboards the gleaming
aluminium front half
of a B36
pokes out from the wall,

engines idling. Useful. she said
for all those slicing jobs
and smiled through mentholated smoke
determined I could see
to play it cool. After all
it's not every day
a bomber drops by.

The crew it appeared had gone
down to the pub, would be back
in time for the meatloaf. Did you know
these planes are so long
a railway runs inside?

Later, as you sprawl in your tumultuous bed
of clouds, big radials throbbing,
sore from a night's high revs,
bomb doors hanging ragged,
tail half-shot-away,
the longlegged scanty-clad
Jane on your nose will wearily wink
and enquire if you wish
you'd stayed down with the ground crew.

Factory-fresh and spanking new
last week, you were just ice cream

to the pilots who flew you:
now after a boring night clawing
at high cirrostratus, you're spent,
imperfections in the scheme of things
start to glare and your coveralls
smell of kerosene and sweat.
It was *cold* up there.

Projections

I can't be the only one
whose bedroom curtains
grow faces like those puzzles
in the children's annuals—
nine birds are hidden
among the leaves.
Can you find them all?

When I met you first I thought
This could be my fate, my companion.
Turned out you were just
another bloody duende.

The faces frown their disapproval.

We talk about how
what seemed to be this
is more of that.

Ever noticed how the zigzag
that represents the hair
at the back of Homer Simpson's head
is like the line I stab
with precisely the right knife
to make Sunday's grapefruit fancy?

Elegant doggerel

Here's an instruction:
check your mailbox,
deny all attraction,

disregard sex.
Those in glass houses
keep away from rocks—

just making faces
from the safety
has to suffice.

Even that's risky,
we're so vulnerable.
The place smells musty,

you hear a rumble
and know it's happened
and you're in trouble

of the deepest kind.
All ill wind's bad enough:
faced with this evil wind

you'd have to be so tough,
so truly muscle-bound
humanity would drop off

and leave you lizard-skinned,
impermeable alike to love
and whatever might wound.

Animals at Anna's

LION:
Love from Guy, June 1989 for Mrs Massey,
to whom I give my power
Jackal
Ibis
Hawk
all lurk in the triple mirror
but right now something
makes the choice for me
to be the crayoned ridiculous
lion with a body
like a yellow fifties table
on four black spindly legs,
a tail like a yellow loo brush
and a face with wide eyes a dot nose
and a u-shaped grin from ear to ear
on the front of a tan balloon of a head.
I am seven. I shall grow up to be
an artist and a lover of women.

JACKAL:
I despise lion
roaring, clowning,
clouting his women around,
gulping down easy meat
in a hurry, afraid
of the dark and me
who haunt the city of the dead
fearless
belly to the ground,
only snakes lower. I steal his prey.
There are old jackals, bold jackals
but no old bold jackals.

HAWK:
I accept I shall die young.
There are no old hawks.
Living depends on the clear eye
the sure foot
the strong heart I carry
to the other world.

IBIS:
I am the calm white mystery
straddling two worlds
suddenly gone
for half the year.
High flyer,
companion of spirits.

Is that it, then?

That's it. Finito con. You've had your time,
your chance to sit & talk, and then some.
Too bad a typhoon struck while the clock
was running away with your heart. It broke

long before, so don't come the old sob story—
 this is a girl, remember, who understands history
and furthermore has powers of recall
to rival a camera. No chance at all

of slipping anything past those unflinching
eyes, steady, direct and leading her
straight to your soul's centre like a syringe
taped into a vein. She's out of range

of your offensive armament, has left no chink.
No chance to share her life. You'll get over
the imagined rejection. There was never
 a promise. Accept you drew a blank.

AND HOW

'They're mine' saith the Lord

God came like a dragon in the night
and took into his long mouth
my cock and balls.

As his teeth gently closed
round the root of my scrotum
I understood what he meant, in a way
but I was still afraid and confused.

A whole new world

Sometimes I recognise things in my dreams as mine,
relevant. This morning's was for all the world as if
it had strayed out of someone else's sleep. It bore
absolutely no resemblance to any office equipment
I have ever laid eyes on. Yet they called it
a copier. No one says I must get to know
how to use it but I know I will.

How will you get on, Lord?
after Rilke

Will you get Mrs Greenbaum from down the landing
to come in and sweep up the pieces
when I your jug fall in the dark flat?

Will that adopted stray that goes through life
in a cloud of loose fur condescend
to lick up me the milk spilled
on the old brown lino?

Will you get a goal, a motivation?
And what will you put on, then,
to go down into the streets
& try to make an honest buck?

And if you find a reason to return
to an empty place with no-one to call to
Honey, I'm home

will you ever again bother to change your street shoes
for me your old velvet slippers?

Why are there colours?

We write in blue or black (occasionally green)
on white or whitish paper
about colours.

None of us is wearing yellow
pink
or orange.

Are there other colours
we don't know about?

Is cold or hot or sad or bored a colour?

In America cardinals are common little birds
bright red all over. Why?

Once God had found a proper bird colour
(white or black or browny)
why make them in other colours?

Of course, God is not a person.

The real mystery is deeper—why we have eyes
that see wavelengths as colours. Stuff like that.

THE MIRANDA'S HONDA POEMS

Sorcerer's Honda

A 90cc bike
with no front wheel
is going nowhere
in Miranda's back garden.

Small trees have grown through it
so it's a standing invitation
to get on and ride
into the ground.

The bruja Honda pretext

I forget now upon what rococo alibi
the import of this bizarre
bramble-clad red
objet trouvé so much depends

how long ago bum up
its wheel-free front fangs
first knelt to pray their hungry
crayfish way into this hard
couchgrass-deep heart

and the arms of the young
Arthur Rackham shrub began
to claw around the hub of the rear
o chrome, o aluminium!
It will for ever lunge, crash
deep into the surf
a jet boat to transport
the soul of its rider
invisible Miranda
to the underworld.

The proper employment for a poet is saving his own life

Print from seven to twenty-two
I woke telling myself
in order to solve the page number problem
with the pamphlet

and in five hours
I shall be looking without seeing them
at the mid-morning cars and vans
passing below the uncomplicated
vertical blinds in my therapist
Kate's first floor consulting room

presumably because
in the mind of the Buddha
I am one of the innumerable things
he has vowed to save.

Our existence is a poem
we are writing in collaboration
with all the others who contribute
to the texture of our life.

And the purpose of the Kwik-Fit fitters
who let me keep running my car
and shout as they work
is the same one as the blackbird's
—to give texture—
 but we all have to do it
for our own reasons.

What his Sunday morning coldness means

He wants predator and flower
to share an outline, almost inseparable
as the wolfish crone and the red-cloak
Sunday shop-girl in the velvet choker
who looks away. Two lovers travelling
in opposite directions hot & cold
like mixing water tapped into a bath.

He had loved in the athletic anatomies of the young
the distinct predictable proof
of god's engineering: those tabs
of muscle above the pelvis
but the parents had shouted him down
into the papers, out of the art room.

And he doesn't say
as he passes her stylish plate
bearing crumpets that smile with butter
Take, eat, this is my life
that I freely gave for you,
that would have been
a different article had I not,
but he means it.

Hints for travellers

I drove an unfenced road
open to the grail
as a wide flower is open
to the idea of summer rain,
but sure this road would end
deep in an ancient forest.

A corn-green bird
crowned rose-red
surprised me
skimming tall maize alongside.

A kilometre on
a thought of him again
made him appear,
though it could be another
that laughed as it slipped
touching flame between birch-saplings.

Now I know the wildwood
that shelters the entrance
to that Other World
need not be glass-dark
heavy and silent
but is just as likely
a gold thicket, slight, bright
and ringing with birds.

God may well be a bird

You go to these boot sales
and see all this stuff
people used to think they needed:
food processors; ugly brown crockery;
heated rollers; Harold Robbins novels,
especially 'The Betsy';
The Observer's Book of Birds.

Did we all have a time when we wanted to tell
a thrush from a lady blackbird?

It's rained pretty well all day in Devon.
From the window of our B&B cottage I watch
a medium-sized brown bird on the lawn
listening and looking for worms. Or snails.
She doesn't care what we call her.
She concentrates on being herself. Or God.
Behind me on the bookshelves, gathering dust,
stands the Reader's Digest Book of the Supernatural.

The magic levels

Here the sea is out of sight
and yet the sense of the sea
is never silent. These lands
recall its run
and wash. Umbilical hills
round as a belly
were maybe islands,
maiden castles, tors.
What matters here
where silver, spilled
in muddy tyre-tracks,
cools to broken bars of sky,
is to entertain
the possibility of legends.

SULA, GUNWOMAN

1 ⁺ Another kind of mirror

As if my head were an old wireless
seldom tuned to the place
that all day and all night plays,

my ears at certain times
like a dream undisturbed
can catch a glimpse

of the private burble
my soul puts on the air
for its own purposes,

so I forgive for what we try to ignore—
relentless from the back of the bus
their self-absorbed verbal blur—

Pete and Bill, Bill and Rose,
Rose and Bob, Bob and Pete,
whom I could kill otherwise.

2 ⁺ Roleplayer

Secretly now I sense
I am gunman for the group, dark sister
licensed to dress in black and be despised
but needed.
With a handful of red feathers
I could simulate a murder.

3 · On the isthmus

We entered the town by the gate
on the sunny side (south I suppose)
where we would buy pineapple later.

Like a cut-out row of tulips
the walls overhang the sparkle
of water that laps

either side. Palm spikes
top the battlements.
Black-clad bikers

in icecream enjoyment
sat on rocks among pink thrift
looking quite innocent.

4 · The assassin addresses her silver child

Swaddled in a stolen napkin
you can wait in the hotel safe,

the cool white linen
firm and smooth as the lateness
of spring in the high passes.

5 · Autobiography

My thoughts feel tight this morning,
flat and black but a trifle constricting. Flirt
with the desk clerk—
not too much—he may be useful later.
Early on, while I had yet to place my first story,
I wanted a way to support myself and still have time to write.
Many girls I knew in that state
moved into the sex industry.
You have to remember I'm so good
I work only two days a week,
so I still had the energy.

An admirer gave me my first pistol as protection.
I soon found I had a knack, grew used to more money
than I got from the magazines. I can feel the hard shape,
like a flat black automatic thought, tucked in the back
of the waistband under my jacket. The spare clip
a weight in my pocket I don't need.
Better travel light or be prepared? I walk tense
to be sure it won't slip down and give me away,
sit up straight so it doesn't dig in.

It's a new gun, not cheap but untried
and may not be reliable. When I find a Ladies
I can check the safety. I have painted
my eyes and brows into a perfect butterfly to distract
from my corrupt thoughts, my dark lips,
the mulberry lips, that powerful black pout.

6 · Going to Work
for Pat, who wanted to know more

I feed
my Black Mollies
in their big tank

my lovelies
I keep clean

I burn
a little sweetgrass
clears the brain

assume
the lotus position

I pick up
my rings
from the glass table

pack cashmere
to travel well

I put on silk
cool
it likes my skin

take the Glock 8c
lightweight and flat

on the plane
I sit alone
do the breathing

they say
Downey is a shit

soon
I will kill him
they have paid me

I get high
on being clean

7 · A logical conclusion

The pungent grey and blue scribble past
the serene carved mask
on the wall by the window-seat. She tastes
a last trace of lipstick
as she polishes the stainless
slide of her automatic,
left hand holding it steady
on the edge of the table,
right massaging in the good gunoil
with a fingertip wrapped
in thick white cotton, rubbing
spots from the grip. Believing
in what she does makes that
and the action fine.

Train dirt washed from her hair,
a white towelling robe
finishes the drying.
A bag of dry-cleaning
waits by the door, ready to drop off
on the way to a silent confession
at SS. Philip and James,
a reporting back
to her gunsmith,
to the spirit of her shooting instructor
on the use of her talent.

She reassures herself once more
that her system's foolproof,
that there can't be a knock at her door.

8 · Sula dreams of Death her master

Beginning at last the marking
she so rarely takes home,
Adam finally settled and quiet
in the next room, she muses
on her other profession,
how some must be
by bomb or poison, but how
she prefers to be there,
to see them go down
like cattle at an abattoir.

9 · Downey's suit is too tight

How did he know
he would know
the first time he saw this woman?

He thought he just did
what he had to do
to please the boss;
didn't know he loved the boss
or hoped
the boss loved him.

He guesses a lady priest,
sitting alone
—that steady gaze,
the plain cross.
Didn't know
they dressed so well.

He feels an interest,
a frisson; notices
the strong hands.

10 · The assumption of Sula Mackay Bassana

She is White Buffalo Cow Woman Appears,
can be seen far off coming over the sea of prairie.
The ground beats at her approach. Also
the Hare Maiden who dwells in the grey moon,
she can move like smoke. Lepus timidus,
she maintains camouflage in every season
by changing her coat colour. The far-seer,
she likes open country
where she can escape her predators
by running.

11 · The prayer on Downey's amulet

O my heart which I received from my mother,
my heart of my different ages,
do not stand up against me as witness!
Do not create opposition against me among the ancestors!
Do not tip the scales against me, the dung-beetle,
in the presence of the Keeper of the Balance!
Let it not be said when my actions are being judged
that 'the name of the person
for whom this heart scarab was made
has been erased from the registers'!
O let not my heart weigh too much
against the feather of Maat, goddess of truth,
and let me be accepted by Osiris.
I have faithfully served Khepri the self-created one.
Let my death be only a prologue to rebirth.

12 · Let them become horses of heaven

Make the chosen horses
beautiful with paint,
with the finest bright felt saddles, bronze-fitted,
before we take the mace
and kill them at the grave's edge,
for how would a man live for ever over there
with no horse to mount—
scarlet, black, ochre, white?

INDICES

Extract from feather list 1: Macaw Jacket

Extract from feather list 2: Heron

2514 small scarlet rh sleeve
2515 small scatlet rh sleeve
2516 small scarlet rh sleeve
2517 small scarlet rh sleeve
2518 small scarlet rh sleeve
2519 small scarlet rh sleeve
2520 small scarlet rh sleeve
2521 small scarlet rh sleeve
2522 small scarlet rh sleeve
2523 small scarlet rh sleeve
2525 small scarlet rh sleeve
2526 small scarlet rh sleeve
2527 small orange rh sleeve
2528 small orange rh sleeve
2529 small orange rh sleeve
2530 small orange rh sleeve
2531 small orange rh sleeve
2532 small orange rh sleeve
2533 small orange rh sleeve
2534 small orange rh sleeve
2535 small orange rh sleeve
2536 small turquoise rh sleeve

30498 small grey lower belly
30499 small grey lower belly
30500 small grey lower belly
30501 small grey lower belly
30502 small grey lower belly
30503 small grey lower belly
30504 small grey lower belly
30505 small grey lower belly
30506 small grey lower belly
30507 small white lower belly
30508 small white lower belly
30509 small white lower belly
30510 small white lower belly
30511 small white lower belly
30512 small white lower belly
30513 small white right upper leg
30514 small white right upper leg
30515 small white right upper leg
30516 small white right upper leg
30517 small white right upper leg
30518 small white right upper leg
30519 small white right upper leg
30520 small white right upper leg
30521 small white right upper leg
30522 small white right upper leg

Mr Bird, Flying Coat Maker

Observe the colours.
Grey is a colour.
God is a spirit.
We're hovering
on the edge of meaning here.

Take one hundred and four
macaws. Pluck. Sort.
Sew sew sew sew sew.

Put something on your fingers
to heal the bleeding. Fly.

Must have been like a rainbow edition
of the snowstorm
from plucking the Christmas goose
in the parrot-coat-maker's house
when the hunters came back
with the birds
and the orders came in.
Feather cola.

Or Mr Feathercote
in the square day after day
coaxing them with bread
and stealing a feather or two
to go in his bag.
Slate is a colour.
So is dove.

THE PALÆOGRAPHY POEMS
[a translation in progress, from clay tablet fragments
found in an excavated granary on the Chinese/Turkish border]

The Three Men are in Love with a River Called Onecandleandanotherthing

Three women in veils.
A man leading a tiger under the arch on a leash.
The gatekeeper wears a uniform, ill-fitting but becoming.
Drug dealers have a stall by the dead tree. No watchmen come.
The magistrate is a drug user. All the bureaucrats are in
the timber trade. Forestry was the basis of the community
but the old skills are dying.

A Hurricane Exhumes the Body of a Worker in the Forest by the Acandleandanotherthing River

When a hurricane exhumes the body of a woodman in the forest
the master congratulates the apprentice woodman for the felled
tree: 'You could learn to (be trusted to) go to buy horses in my stead'.
In reality he is a horseman (fast rider). The workman imagines
an alternative universe: a portcullis and serving-men—two chefs
working in partnership; an enormous cooking-pot [philanthropy;
Lord Bountiful] and knightly games [rituals or jousting—the
quintain]; [room to improvise] underworked servants going to the
food store; flying kites; having an easy life.
He the king/buddha founding new forests; founding, and caring
for, a new race/tribe/society/settlement.
Collapse of structures; the gallows; a pile of logs. Lazy servants no
longer flying kites. He himself the only one now who flies a kite
and has an easy time.
He looks up through the new leaves. The clouds are a window
to the sun. Trees grow and are cut down quickly [symbol of com-
pletion] He builds a communal living-house, feels humble and
acknowledges his great good fortune.

War at Sea

1. A single sail, sailing away, watchful and 'hard-rowed'. A famous pirate, Cutlass Hero. A whole bunch of ships of all sizes in a mêlée. Rockets. Explosions. A calm (no wind). Many deaths (widows made). Ill fortune. Cutlass Hero ('famous pirate') survives. Few others do. He tries to blow up the fortress but the commander makes his getaway. The trap closes empty, on only a log! They mock him to fury, he becomes red faced, overturns the castle/house (condominium). There are funerals (wailing, prayers, ashes). There is looting ('soldiers come, shoot, sit down' i.e. pillage). Snake-fangs, poison. No wind. The insane priest beats a drum. From the ruins (empty houses?) a little man builds a fighting-boat (i.e. the cycle begins again?)

2. The furious warlord shoots (into the air) and no-one has any fun. There are cats (? Or racing-camels) No wind (i.e. sails are, or remain, furled) An explosion causes the magic lamp by the hearth to explode. There is a medium-sized explosion which may grow bigger.

3 A tent/cottage/flimsy village. Dragonfly. Below 'low-flying passenger kites—no ponies allowed' many pony-riders come. They prepare for battle. Ships are sunk. Formal dances take place in the street. Flags at half-mast. The furious warlord [Major-General] shoots into the air. He is serious. No-one has any fun. They prepare for battle. The village is deserted. The kite-flying-ground is blown up. The riders return (depart). Shots are fired into the air. It may get worse.

4. Ships are sunk for no reason. Houses are put onto ox-carts. Wooden arches. Folding chairs in front of a flickering blue lamp in a corner of the desert. Listen to the Hero talking (too?) loudly to the whole community through the magic lamp on the hearth. A series of dramas 'Zor-ro'. A rootless man chasing wild horses.
The man builds a house. He is an inventor ('a cunning man'). He shoots well (trees are cut down). Prosperity/good fortune. A successful conclusion.

Oxen walk abroad (= the fields grow larger). Fortification (of the flimsy houses) occurs. Here comes a (whole) phalanx of crazed Major-Generals firing into the air.
The Major-General calms a little, though he still enjoys spoiling people's fun and shooting into the air.

The Shop Selling Statuettes and Gowns

Forest cut down
birds fly away
logs in a pile
deer fight
floods follow

under the wooden arch
we commiserate
by the pile of logs
we lament together
the absence of hawks
the chess players
enjoy companionship
by the log pile
their houses are in ruins
All the village is in ruins
[no birds sing]
There used to be birdsong in the municipal zoo.
Now there is only a turnstile and some logs.
Even the spilled peanuts attract no sparrows
by the turnstile.
Bamboo; logs; caged tigers.

For Gerald Stern

You talked about waiting for the dead plants
to arrive in the post, and now I'm also doing it,
carefully unfolding the brown paper
from the thick root hairs like a broom
clumped with grainy stuff. It reminds me
of bringing up iron filings like coffee grounds
in the bowl at the old hospital
the Americans built.

And the clear plastic pierced like lace.

There's the baked earth tablet
hardly cracked at all among that broken clay
in the bottom of the enormous pit
lined with pottery like a bottle a thief could hide in.

Pictures of wine jars and small chariots
and men in plaited wigs. Here strides a
military taskmaster You can hear
the creak of his dry boots
on the broken stones. In his pocket
a picture of larches and cedars,
the bill for his son's pony. He understands
corn and the weather. A dusty assistant
follows with folding scales. His dreams
are of castles and tigers; of fast ships.

Epitome:
an Ashbourne visit index

4 wheel drives

Ankles, cold

Bed, goosefeather
Bowls, emptying of

Cars, stuck

Failure, *see* Living vans,
   search for
Fair Hill

Gravel
Grit
Halter top, black
Heels, naked, use of as spurs
Honey, colour of

Impromptuness, *see also*
   Spur (of the moment)
Impulsiveness

Jam, vehicle
Lakeland, naming of
Living vans, search for

Moment, spur of the

Paddling
Pebbles
Ponies up out of river, urging of
Pony-riding posture, boys'
Posture, riding, straight legged

Riding, bareback
Rocks, dark, shiny

Shade
Skewbald
Splosh
Spongebrush, long-handled
Spur *see under* Heels; Moment

Towel, absence of need for
Trainers, soaked
Turf

Vans, blue Transit, washing of
Vehicle registration plates, Irish,
   new

Water, horse-washing
Weir, clear
Wet hooves on stone
Wheelspin
Whinnying

THE BEING NORTHEUROPEAN POEMS

From his panelled room

the man in the thick shirt
who may be Stead Steadman himself
gazes out at the opposite flats
under North European white sky,
an emperor exiled from Rome
expecting snow. Did he express a view
about middle-class housing? Is he angered
that his mother lacked vision, his father conviction?

An index to the biographical fragment
Being Northeuropean *by Stead Steadman*

The Identification of Parts poems

1. (see at 10A below)—this shd also be in my small cloth-covered 1999 notebook:
[THE POEM ABOUT HOW] Each part of me carries an identical passport (except maybe as to Occupation*)

2. Passport photos

3. The photo sessions

4. The missing part (see 6)

(0. Mr Bird, coatmaker)

5. Who didn't come on passport photo day? (Why not?) What did he (she) do instead?

6. The one to whom physical courage / cowardice is an issue (knife)

7. The 'failed' painter—not failed, just decided to break off developing for a while
HOW WOULD HE START (TO WRITE) A POEM . . . ?

10a. EACH MEMBER CARRIES AN IDENTICAL PASSPORT (except maybe as to Occupation*) Despite times when the autonomous parts of me reveal their unique (personal traits)ness, when most of us went to get our passport photos done, we all washed & combed our hair & wore a dark suit, so that's no help.
Each can and does produce [from his charcoal suit's top pocket a photo (along the general lines of that painting of a man looking at the back of his head in a mirror by the guy who did the train coming out of a fireplace) that is recognisably him and not the others, so they can be identified] but only as they are leaving . . .
Oh, forget it!

* where it says variously
Agent Provocateur
Specialist garment maker
[under 15: no separate passport required]
Mystic; shaman; jester; priest; juggler; monk; ingénue; teacher
Conceptual artist
Actor
Novelist
Indigent (no passport required? or offered?)
Assassin

Seriously, though, the parts of me I need to get to talk to:
Daughter
Painter/artist
The Uncomprehending Part
Schoolteacher/drudge
The Part of Faith
The Manager
The Intuitive/seer
The Good husband/father/friend

An index to the driftwood project

Index

PAPER SPECIFICATION / POLEMIC

The Five Seasons 'Original' recycled paper (110 gsm) used for this book is manufactured from one hundred per cent pre-consumer RCF (recovered fibre) sourced from scrap chiefly generated during printing and converting operations in the UK, with some addition of 'mill broke'.

No post-consumer fibre has been specified for this paper. This is because no paper mill in the UK currently manufactures quality recycled publishing papers using UK-sourced post-consumer fibre. Some all- or part-recycled publishing papers made in the UK *do* use MDIP (a market de-inked pulp made from post-consumer paper) but this is *imported*—principally from the USA and to a lesser extent from France. Publishers are being encouraged by various campaigns to specify post-consumer recovered fibre in UK-manufactured book papers but this is *not* reducing the amount of waste printed paper dumped in British landfill sites. The production of these 'environmentally-friendly' papers depends on long-distance pulp shipments.

The Waste & Resources Action Programme (WRAP — www.wrap.org.uk) published a major report in January 2005 on the feasibility of resolving this problem by building a pulp mill in the UK capable of producing the required post-consumer RCF pulp: *Market De-Inked Pulp Facility Pre-Feasibility Study* (ISBN 1-84405-142-0). Its findings suggest that a British MDIP facility is unlikely to be built in the near future because of various economic factors (and no British paper mill 'in the printings and writings sector' has 'shown an immediate interest in direct investment in the proposed MDIP plant').

So for the present Five Seasons Press has decided that the best policy is to promote awareness of this regrettable situation and to continue to use UK pre-consumer RCF rather than US post-consumer RCF in Five Seasons recycled papers. Five Seasons also prefers to specify a one hundred per cent furnish of these locally-recovered fibres rather than combine them with Forest Stewardship Council virgin fibres that, as likely as not, come from Uruguayan eucalyptus pulped in Morocco. Five Seasons Press agrees with WRAP's argument that the promotion of recycled paper *per se* is the critical issue. Improved facilities and options will only become economically viable when the demand for recycled papers (whether pre-consumer or post-consumer) increases.

It is of course much more difficult for a large publishing house than for Five Seasons to specify paper of this quality and (relative) probity. One of the many benefits of small-scale publishing.

Glenn Storhaug, publisher